Spitting Distance

Mark Pajak

smith|doorstop

Published 2016 by
smith|doorstop Books
The Poetry Business
Bank Street Arts
32-40 Bank Street
Sheffield S1 2DS

ISBN 978-1-910367-68-1

Designed and Typeset by Utter
Printed by Biddles Books

Acknowledgements

With thanks to Buzzwords for commending 'The Lemon Game'
in the 2014 Cheltenham Poetry Competition; The Poetry Society
for commending 'Cat on the Tracks' in the 2014 National Poetry
Competition; The Bridport Prize for awarding 'Spitting Distance' first
place in the 2016 Poetry competition; *Magma* for printing 'Learning to
Read' and *The Long White Thread of Words: Poems for John Berger* for
which 'Brood' was a commission. Finally to New Writing North for a 2016
Northern Writers Award.

With personal thanks to Suzannah Evans, for all her hard work, to Michael
Symmons Roberts, for his invaluable guidance, and to Carol Ann Duffy,
for her belief in me. Also to my family and friends for all their unwavering
support.

smith|doorstop Books are a member of Inpress:
www.inpressbooks.co.uk. Distributed by Central Books Ltd.,
99 Wallis Road, London E9 5LN

The Poetry Business gratefully acknowledges the support
of Arts Council England.

Supported by
**ARTS COUNCIL
ENGLAND**

Contents

To Mum and Dad
for all your stories and love

After Closing Time
(for Joe)

We head to the edge of town,
to the black river and old stone bridge.

Two boys full of vodka,
tipping side to side like flames.

And for a laugh, we climb
the railing and hang from our arms.

Below in the deep, two boys
peer up at us over their feet.

Like drops of water
we are gathering ourselves to fall.

One of us says, *You go first*,
and we echo this back and forth.

We are here for a very long time.
Years in fact. I marry. Divorce.

You skip all that, become a father.
We see less and less of each other.

Now we are what the world
considers 'men'. Which is to say

we've learnt that falling is inevitable.
Yet here we are still, side by side,

two boys way past closing time,
holding on until the other lets go.

Brood

... and in their glance was permanence
– John Berger

At sixteen, I did a day's work
on an egg farm.
A tin shed the size of a hanger.

Inside its oven dark
two thousand stacked cages,
engines of clatter and squawk.

My job, to pass a torch
through the bars for the dead hens
and pack them tight into a bin bag.

All the time my mind chanting:
there's only one hen. Just one
ruined hen repeated over and over.

In this way I soothed the sight
of all that caged battery,
their feathers stripped to stems,

their patches of scrotum skin,
their bodies held
in the dead hands of their wings.

But what kept me awake
that hot night in my box room,
as I listened to the brook outside

chew on its stones and the fox's
human scream, was how
those thousand-thousand birds

had watched me. And really
it was me repeated over and over,
set in the amber of their eyes.

Me, the frightened boy in jeans
stiff with chicken shit, carrying
a bin bag full of small movement.

A foot that opened. An eyelid
that unshelled its blind nut.
A beak mouthing a word.

The Lemon Game

Wet yourself in Tesco. Mum's finger bullying your bladder
until the hot purse pops wet in your jeans on the fruit and veg isle.
She tuts and it sounds like a slap. Shakes her head. Dangerous.
You are five years old and together you are buying lemons for the lemon game.

Walk a stranger's distance behind her all the way home. *It's the stink of you*
she says, jeans a honey-rot blot catching stares like wasps, cold as nappy rash
when you reach the flat. Sit still on the kitchen floor like a rabbit
put your eyes front, corners on her. *Here is a sweet apple sweet-thing* she says
drops down a lemon green and yellow like an old bruise.

Palm it up in a bite
wax-skin bursting, wetting you chin to chest, your mouth mulling the red taste
its soft clod nothing like an apple's crunch but she studies your face
referees your face pours over your face like scalding kettle water.
                              You know the rules.
                              It must not screw up like a fist.
                              It must not screw up like a fist.

Tickling the Canal

Believe in the dream... Beware the danger
– Marie-Nicole Ryan

Lured to the canal on her dad's yarn
of Alaska and how he'd tickled fish

from icy rivers. And though this is only Bootle,
Liverpool, and rats wicker in the reeds,

a mallard rasps and a condom eels by
on the current, she thinks herself Inuit

in this northern wind that shivers the water
as a magnet will skitter iron shavings.

So she dips her small hands, motions
as if beckoning and waits for the trout.

But there are no trout. Instead, in the sunk
smoke of algae, sticklebacks scatter

like a shoal of razors. Under the drowned
hull of a bathtub, a pike as long as her arm

slys its snout upwards. The rusty ring
of its gullet ready to slip on a finger.

Spitting Distance

Near Edale, I find a live rifle shell
like a gold seed in the earth.

So I load it into my mouth
and go on walking, the sun

breathing down my neck,
the head of Mam Tor rising

and the path falling like a braid.
So this is what it's like to be a gun;

copper bleeding on the gums,
the domino click in the teeth.

At the blue summit, I look down
with my new perspective

on the warped floor of Derbyshire,
to where a village pools in a valley

and a chimney hangs from the sky
on a white string. And I watch

with hunger the red dot of a car
stop at a crossroads. I suck hard

on the blunt bud, drawing out
its deeper flavour of powder,

smoke down the barrel
of my throat. Then it hits me

that there's another side to this.
And I lay in the warm heather.

A body with a bullet
in its head staring at this sky.

Its clouds blown open.
Its sudden night.

Thin

Collie dog
locked
in a shed
in Toxteth.
Dead.
We shoved
the door in
found him
thin.
A bin bag
of cutlery,
a cider pint
stink. Flies
in the spoons
of his eye sockets.
Scraps of fur
crumbed
with blood.
Empty shelves
of ribs
and the pear stalk
of his penis.
Dead. Until
I touched him
and he whined
like a knife
scraping a plate.
Rattled the rinds
of his tail.

Sweet

Here is a fifteen-year-old dosed to his eyes,
lids half-latched, mouth half-sprung,
half-listening to a wasp dizzy over the bed.

It lands its eyelash legs on his cheek
but after sixteen keys of ket
he doesn't flinch as it draws its point
over lips left ajar, scuttles in
and sketches down the tongue
to hum at the tonsil gag.

Much later a pathologist
will hold out a napkin in explanation,
a wasp's sting there like a broken pencil lead.

But in that moment on the bed
who'd have guessed that wasps
taste sweet? A yellow grape
fresh-picked and still warm from the sun,
its stalk pinning the boy's breath
to the throat, the raw strawberry muscle.

Into the Mudflats

She walked from Ipswich.
Followed the Orwell

here, where its mouth
breathes out sea.

And she could show you
in her camera

how the last mile of banks
lost distinction.

Became this grey area
between land and water.

These river margins
ridged like a thumbprint;

waves of silt
crested with pale grass.

Their troughs
full of a deep porridge

where only stink rises;
a salty sewer reek

that even on days like this,
empty of wind,

reaches far inland.
It is beautiful.

That's what she thought.
That's why she left the path

and tried to bound
ridge to ridge

towards the snapshot
of a cormorant on a rock.

And when her foot
missed, her leg dipped

like a spoon in soup.
Then clamped.

And she pulled at the grass
and unlaced white roots.

Groped the earth
and found herself

kneading dough.
Screamed heat

up her throat as cold
swallowed her knees.

And she sank with the sun
to her waist.

Then the melting daylight
slicked on the mudflats

so that, for a moment,
she waded in quicksilver.

And she stopped screaming
because it *was* beautiful.

So bright her torso
blacked out,

became flat and simple.
And she just stood there,

a stencil on the wet shine.
Like the half-sunk

silhouettes on all those signs.
All those luminous

warning signs
put up after the search.

Camping on Arran, 1992

Dad, you had shared with me your sleeping bag.
And we lay like hands held in one pocket.
When the dark flickered and a pause before

thunder; a sound like the sky waking.
And waking with it, I trembled; trapped,
a boy in a storm, in this tight space

ripe with your sleeping man's body.
But when the canvas flared again
white with a hem of shadow grass,

you were awake and counting
down the seconds to thunder.
And I, listening, was struck still.

As each count became less
– the storm brighter, louder –
I could feel a closeness

like breath in the air.
And I fell asleep
as rain would fall; soft,

then in a rush.
You counting us
into the eye.

A Hand

No teacher in sight when the boy
smacks you in the face and, inside,
your head blows its bulb.

The playground continues
its tangle of sound without you;
the chitter of shoes, scuff of talk

and when the bell rings,
it empties. Quiet comes
to crowd the small pile of you.

Then the rain; a tap at the eyelids.
You're hugged by damp clothes.
Your shoulder shook by cold.

When you come-to
it's unclear how much time
has bled onto the concrete.

Beside you, sugared in the wet
and curled like a dead spider,
is a hand. But you're concussed.

Thoughts thread
like a coat done-up wrong.
You don't realise the hand is yours.

So when it unfurls to touch here,
the temple where it hurts,
you say *thank you* out loud.

Fence

I am the city boy on a school trip amazed
by this distance; Cheshire tiled green
with farmland and a blue sky that opens
in my chest. I've wandered off, curious
of this field, its strange crop of white hummocks
– a herd of sun drunk cows. I hear the fence
sizzle before I see it. Then it's there,
its posts like frets of a guitar. Each signs'

Do Not Touch, enough to make me want to.
I hover my hand. Feel a change in weather.
Years from now I'll try to think of my first
kiss – and my mind will blow a fuse, recall
this fingertip, this warm lip of metal
and the stone smooth moment of my stopped heart.

Oil

My torch on in the garage
where a bucket holds a black disc
laminated with light.

It could be polished leather
if it wasn't for those fumes
like a motorway in summer.

I prod the bucket with my foot
and the disc tilts
then licks the insides.

Something breaks the surface.
So I dip my hand,
the oil cold as cream,

and lift the sunken thing,
solid and furry
like a gnawed corn on the cob.

A drowned rat, his body saturated,
emptied of colour
as if switched off.

His swollen eyes tinted
and the spike of his tail leaking,
each drop dilating on the floor.

Later, the white soap in the bathroom
grows a thick grey coat.
The towel a Rorschach print.

Then in bed all I can think is oil
like an eel down the throat,
rolling to a bowling ball in the stomach

and taking root in the soiled lungs,
as I reach for the lamp
and seal myself in black.

Dear Neighbour in the Flat Above

last night I mistook you for falling snow.
In bed I heard my ceiling purr as if
collecting your weight, as though you settled
up there in perfect layers. Then I dreamt
your flat really did fill with soft powder;
an empty table took on a white cloth,
a wood floor heaped to a shag carpet,
a bed beneath a growing feathered quilt.

But when the ceiling started to shiver
I woke. Your noise grown heavy. And then I
realised that there were two of you up there,
making heat. Not grains of snow gathering
on your skins but rain. And my room felt cold.
Its pale bulb flickered. Plaster drifted down.

Known in Passing

I knew summer in New Hampshire.
In the dawn when I walked
in the woods. I knew summer

in the slow sun that opened
between the fir trees. In the blades
of grass set beneath a quartz mist

and tinselled with dew.
I knew summer in the air I drank
cold as if from a night chilled glass

and even in the clod of earth
that opened its eyes, became a rabbit
and slalomed for its hole.

But I didn't know summer
in the bear. In the grizzly
that swayed out of the brush

and stood before me, claws
slotted in the ground. The bear
that sniffed my stiff hand,

her snout nettled maybe by the stink
of a teabag I'd used hours ago.
The bear that dabbed my thumb

with the hot belt of her tongue
and then prowled away,
her felted bulk trailing a dark scent,

the crumbling incense of caves.
The bear that left without a sound
and her smell disbanding

so that you wouldn't even know.
But I knew. And I felt
cold, as though my body

had left summer. And when my biting
teeth released the red leaf of my tongue,
my mouth filled with autumn.

Last Word

My mother says when they tell her
the walnut under her breast is cancer,
or when she meets a stranger in her mirror,
she'll pick a cold night and an empty beach.

She says she'll walk in, North Sea
clenching at her calves until the water
lifts her on its black palm. Then eyes closed,
she'll listen to the rinse in her ears

as the chill sets to work. Finally,
when she feels herself fading,
she'll blow her last breath on a word.
But that word, she says, is her secret.

And I am left imagining all of it.
How the cold will erode her, shed her skins,
unspool each bone to the last thread
of marrow, peel the onion layers of the skull

until she is just a mouth. And I imagine
not what she will say but how the word
must feel. For a moment its last syllable
on the tongue solid as a pearl inside her shell.

Learning to Read
(for Paul)

Beside me, my father
home from the bread factory
fingers gloved in flour
and closed on a belt,
an unbuckled hoof of leather.

I am mealing my teeth,
unable to pick out words
from these black seams
over the pages.
Soon he'll tell me to turn
from the book and, instead,
he'll teach me to brace, to shut.

It's a skill I'll master
before anyone learns I need
a pair of glasses, but today
you can still read it in my face
as the air is licked with flour.

West Tower Fire, Liverpool

Look up. Ignore the stacks
of   glowing   windows

and   this   high-rise
could be a long jetty

into the night, the sky
rippling   at   its   edges

and smoking like a lake
before   dawn.

Listen. Ignore the sirens
and that crackle could be

morning rain on water.
And that man on the roof

just   a   swimmer,
pulling   himself   out

onto the jetty's length
and running down towards

land. Close your eyes
and   this   red   heat

is the sun rising, this lighter
just a pebble in your hand.

My Dead Grandmother

Here is a rope-swing; its blue plait slung
from a branch. Sat there on its knot,
bare feet planted on the riverbank, is gran.

Stood beside her, my dad watches the river
– its spate frayed white on small rocks –
his eyes black pebbles under thick glasses.

But gran's eyes are full of distance, watching
nothing. Her gown breathes-in the breeze,
and her hospice reek, that chemical rot,

meets my father's face thick as damp cloth.
But he says nothing. Just lets the river whisper
its shush of water. Then he gives his *wee mammy*

a push. The swing halves the air like paper.
And as she moves away, her weight
just enough to crack the rope's long spine,

my dad, left behind on the riverbank,
is both the man watching the swing go
and the boy aching for the swing back.

First time my father set a Mousetrap

I thought it was some slender creature.
Its wafer of belly, steel lip, the coiled meeting of its jaw.
I remember how it was loaded with stillness
as if ready to bolt. How dad pulled back its snout
easy as a wishbone and it screamed
like a rusty hinge. How he locked it agape,
placed a cherry on its one tooth and left it there.

Then later in my cot, the night loose from its hole
and the whole house under a lid of quiet, a snap
tripped my ears. Slow and sleepy
my child's mind unfolded and recalled
that poor slender creature, which now
must have bitten itself free. And I lay there, relieved,
my pulse scurrying in the small tunnels of my wrist.

Cat on the Tracks

He wore the night in his fur, sat on a rung
between the rails, tail wisping like smoke

as a distant train split the air along its seam.
Its coming headlight laid down track

and placed an opal into each black seed
of the cat's eyes, every blink slow as an eclipse.

Soon the white light pinned him, the only drop
of night left as vibration turned the rails to mercury.

But there was no give in the cat, no flex anywhere
but his tail. And for a moment their roles reversed,

as though it were the train facing the inevitable cat,
the end of the line. The world lit up like a page

and the train a sentence before the full-stop.

3O years
of smith|doorstop poets

Moniza Alvi, David Annwn, Simon Armitage, Jane Aspinall, Ann Atkinson, David Attwooll, Anne-Marie Austin, Sally Baker, Mike Barlow, Kate Bass, Paul Batchelor, Suzanne Batty, Zeina Hashem Beck, Chris Beckett, Peter Bennet, Catherine Benson, Gerard Benson, Paul Bentley, Sujata Bhatt, David Borrott, Nina Boyd, Maxwell Boyle, Sue Boyle, Carol Brierly, Susan Bright, Carole Bromley, Sue Butler, Peter Carpenter, James Caruth, Liz Cashdan, Dennis Casling, Julia Casterton, Claire Chapman, Debjani Chatterjee, Linda Chase, Geraldine Clarkson, Stephanie Conn, Stanley Cook, Bob Cooper, Jennifer Copley, Julia Copus, Rosaleen Croghan, Tim Cumming, Paula Cunningham, Simon Currie, Duncan Curry, Ann Dancy, Emma Danes, Peter Daniels, Peter Daniels Luczinski, Joyce Darke, Jonathan Davidson, Kwame Dawes, Owen Davis, Julia Deakin, Nichola Deane, Steve Dearden, Patricia Debney, Mike DiPlacido, Maura Dooley, Tim Dooley, Jane Draycott, Basil du Toit, Christy Ducker, Carol Ann Duffy, Sue Dymoke, Stephen Duncan, Suzannah Evans, Michael Farley, Rebecca Farmer, Nell Farrell, Catherine Fisher, Janet Fisher, Anna Fissler, Andrew Forster, Katherine Frost, Sam Gardiner, Adele Gèras, Sally Goldsmith, Yvonne Green, David Grubb, Harry Guest, Robert Hamberger, David Harmer, Sophie Hannah, John Harvey, Jo Haslam, Geoff Hattersley, Jeanette Hattersley, Selima Hill, John Hilton, Andrea Holland, Holly Hopkins, Sian Hughes, Keith Jafrate, Lesley Jefferies, Chris Jones, Mimi Khalvati, John Killick, Jenny King, Mary King, Stephen Knight, Judith Lal, John Lancaster, Peter Lane, Michael Laskey, Kim Lasky, Brenda Lealman, Tim Liardet, Katherine Lightfoot, Semyon Izrailevich Lipkin, John Lyons, Maitreyabandhu, Paul Matthews, Eleanor Maxted, John McAuliffe, Michael McCarthy, Rachel McCarthy, Patrick McGuinness, Kath McKay, Paul McLoughlin, Hugh McMillan, Ian McMillan, Allison McVety, Julie Mellor, Hilary Menos, Paul Mills, Hubert Moore, Kim Moore, David Morley, Sarah Morris, Blake Morrison, Paul Munden, Daljit Nagra, Dorothy Nimmo, Stephanie Norgate, Christopher North, Carita Nystrom, Sean O'Brien, Padraig O'Morain, Mark Pajak, Nigel Pantling, Alan Payne, Pascale Petit, Stuart Pickford, Ann Pilling, Jim Pollard, Wayne Price, Simon Rae, Irene Rawnsley, Ed Reiss, Neil Roberts, Marlynn Rosario, Padraig Rooney, Jane Routh, Peter Sansom, Tom Sastry, Michael Schmidt, Myra Schneider, Rosie Shepperd, Lemn Sissay, Felicity Skelton, Catherine Smith, Elspeth Smith, Joan Jobe Smith, Cherry Smytb, Martin Stannard, Pauline Stainer, Paul Stephenson, Mandy Sutter, Matthew Sweeney, Diana Syder, David Tait, Pam Thompson, Dennis Travis, Susan Utting, Stephen Waling, Martin Wiley, Tony Williams, Ben Wilkinson, Andrew Wilson, David Wilson, River Wolton, Sue Wood, Anna Woodford, Cliff Yates, Luke Samuel Yates

Laureate's Choice 2015 pamphlets
still available from the Poetry Business

David Borrott | Nichola Deane | Rachel McCarthy | Wayne Price

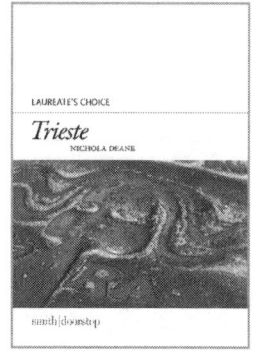

This is a varied but coherent collection, tender, imaginative and clear-eyed. – Carol Ann Duffy

A poet both sophisticated and lyrically charged who deploys imagery that is both precise and daring. – Carol Ann Duffy

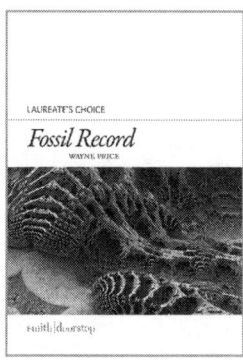

Here are bold poems in a collection that is much more than the sum of its mesmerising parts.
— Carol Ann Duffy

A remarkable new poet who is intelligent, insightful, imaginative and utterly assured.
— Carol Ann Duffy

£7.50 each or all 4 for £20
www.poetrybusiness.co.uk

Thirty poems to celebrate thirty years of Poetry Business pamphlets

Founded in 1986 on an Enterprise Allowance, the Poetry Business was based for twenty years in a Victorian Arcade in Huddersfield, with poets Peter Sansom and Janet Fisher as co-directors. After Janet's retirement, the poet Ann Sansom took over as co-director and the business moved to its present offices in Bank Street Arts in Sheffield.

For all of those 30 years, we have been publishing pamphlets of one shape or another, starting with Simon Armitage's first published poems in *Human Geography*, right up until the present day with our Laureate's Choice pamphlets by four up-and-coming poets chosen by Carol Ann Duffy.

30 at thirty brings you thirty poems, one from each of the thirty years of the Poetry Business.

£5

www.poetrybusiness.co.uk